CW00340284

LONDON ROUTEMASTERS

IN THE LATE 1970s AND EARLY 1980s

MIKE RHODES

AMBERLEY

First published 2020

Amberley Publishing
The Hill, Stroud
Gloucestershire, GL5 4EP

www.amberley-books.com

Copyright © Mike Rhodes, 2020

The right of Mike Rhodes to be identified as
the Author of this work has been asserted in
accordance with the Copyrights, Designs and
Patents Act 1988.

ISBN 978 1 4456 9388 0 (print)
ISBN 978 1 4456 9389 7 (ebook)

All rights reserved. No part of this book may be
reprinted or reproduced or utilised in any form
or by any electronic, mechanical or other means,
now known or hereafter invented, including
photocopying and recording, or in any information
storage or retrieval system, without the permission
in writing from the Publishers.

British Library Cataloguing in Publication Data.
A catalogue record for this book is available from
the British Library.

Typesetting by Aura Technology and Software
Services, India. Printed in the UK.

Introduction

Numerous books have been written about the London Routemaster, documenting its development in the mid-1950s and describing its years of mainstream operation in everyday service in the Capital, from June 1959 until their final demise in December 2005 (excepting heritage route operation). Eventually numbering some 2,760 examples, they could be found operating from virtually every London bus garage, both in the Red Central Area and the Green Country Area. There was the original sixty-four-seat, 27-foot 6-inches long version and the seventy-two-seat, 30-foot long variation, the latter having first been introduced into service with a small batch of twenty-four buses in 1961, but not put into full production until 1965. The country fleet also possessed coach-seated versions in the form of the RMC (27 feet 8 inches long) and the RCL (30 feet long).

Following the use of a number of early RMs as 'Trainers' on a variety of routes, they were first used to convert trolleybus routes to motorbus operation, from stage 4 of the conversion programme. This initially involved converting a number of routes in East London in November 1959, which were operated out of Poplar and West Ham garages. The programme of conversions was concluded with stage 14 in May 1962, when RMs were introduced to Fulwell garage and Isleworth trolleybus depot was closed. Thereafter they replaced the variants of the RT family, such as the last of the RTL and RTW types, in the mid to late 1960s.

The Routemaster was especially designed for ease of maintenance, a feature that was ably demonstrated when the buses visited the Aldenham bus overhaul works. Here the bodies were separated from the chassis and each of the two components progressed through the works at a different pace. At the end of the line the overhauled chassis was married up with a different body from the one that the bus had arrived with. To enable this system to work smoothly, what was known as a 'Works Float' of bus bodies was created whereby, for long periods of time, certain RM bus numbers did not exist as 'running-units' as the bodies were distributed on a variety of newly overhauled chassis. Only when the 'Works Float' system was abandoned, in the early 1980s, did some of the long-missing running-unit numbers appear on the streets. This practice could easily be discerned when high-numbered RMs could be seen with non-opening upper-deck windows, a feature that was originally confined to the early production models up to RM253.

The pictures included in this portrait were taken on a succession of visits I made to the Capital City between 1976 and 1985. During this time I made extensive use of the 'Red Bus Rover' day ticket (and a handful of 'Go-As-You-Please' multi-day tickets), purchasing no fewer than sixty-nine examples of the thin card day ticket. The first of these cost me just 90 pence and whilst the price had escalated to £2.40 by early 1983, it then dropped in price to £1.80 by the end of my visits. Purchasing one of these tickets was a challenge in itself as they could not be obtained on the buses. Quite often it was convenient to call in at a bus garage where they were always available at the office. This would also present an excuse to enter the premises, although in those days a quick word with the garage foreman was usually sufficient to gain entry to see what gems were lurking inside. Victoria garage was often a good starting point, although I once remember buying my ticket from Middle Row garage early on a Sunday morning. This somewhat antiquated garage (it was closed in August 1981) was crammed full of Routemasters and the counter was difficult to access and hidden behind a small window in one of the garage walls. The occupant of the office was not only surprised to receive a request for a Red Bus Rover but also had difficulty in locating the supply of tickets. Even when they were eventually found, the office clerk had to dust the cobwebs off the stack. Of equal importance in order to navigate oneself around the extensive route system was a copy of the London Buses Route Map, which not only showed the line of the routes but also the terminal points and the location of all sixty-nine Red Bus garages.

At the start of this period the RM fleet was almost intact, with just a few examples having been lost to accidents or incidents. London Country was acquired by the National Bus Company (NBC) on 1 January 1970 and whilst the many green Regents and Routemasters continued to function with that operator for a number of years, the RTs were gradually phased out and virtually all of the RCLs and the majority of the RMCs were eventually acquired by London Transport, although at that time the latter were used mainly as training vehicles. Many of the RCLs and RMLs were overhauled and painted red, although some did fall by the wayside and provided a source of spares for the refurbished buses. London Transport also acquired the majority of the former British European Airways (BEA and latterly BOAC) Routemasters and although a number were briefly used in service from Romford garage, these too largely acted as trainers.

The subject matter has, in the main, been arranged in route number order. Over the period covered by the book I managed to photograph RMs on the vast majority of the routes they operated on. Of the routes which eluded me, a number only saw Routemaster operation on a Sunday and others were 'suffix' letter routes. The most significant omissions are probably the 4 (Archway Station to Waterloo), the 36A (West Kilburn to Brockley Rise), which was operated by the type for twenty-eight years, and the 176 (Willesden Garage to Forest Hill). I could perhaps be forgiven for missing out on the 261 (Barnet to Arnos Grove Station) as RM operation lasted just seven weeks in 1978. Nevertheless, they are depicted working on 125 different routes across the London Transport central area network, with a handful of contrasting Country Area routes thrown in for good measure.

The reader is taken on a tour of the whole of the Red Bus operating network with RMs widely depicted as far apart as Staines on the 117, Harold Hill on the 87, Old Coulsdon on the 59 and at the northerly outpost of Hammond Street on the 279, along with a contrasting variety of locations at all points of the compass in between. The array of layover points was typical of the era. Whilst the Farnborough George & Dragon (which was originally a staging post for horse-drawn carriages) and Chislehurst War Memorial termini were just two examples of scenic settings, these contrasted widely with such obscure bus stands as afforded for the 40 at Herne Hill and for the 140 at Hayes. Unlike in the twenty-first century, local bus stations in London were few and far between, although these did exist at such places as Aldgate, Golders Green, Hounslow, Kingston, Lewisham, Turnpike Lane and Victoria. The period under review also includes the year of HM Queen Elizabeth II's Silver Jubilee, which was marked by London Transport (LT) with the painting of twenty-five Routemasters in an all-over silver livery. These were officially launched into service on 10 April 1977, following a gathering of all twenty-five buses in South Carriage Drive alongside Hyde Park.

The book largely covers what could loosely be termed as the Routemaster's swansong, as many of the type were withdrawn from 1984 onwards and, initially, a lot of these were sold for scrap until, with the advent of bus deregulation on the horizon, it was realised that there was a market for these twenty-five-year-old buses. Indeed deregulation proved a godsend for many Routemasters which found new homes working in Scotland and the provinces.

Blackpool Transport, Burnley & Pendle, Reading Mainline and Southend Transport were just four of the operators who subsequently benefitted from the type. Also, in the Capital the RM was given a new lease of life. Many of the remaining buses were refurbished as from 1986 they became the responsibility of the newly formed London Regional Transport. Under this umbrella they were eventually split amongst a number of newly created operating units, all of which were privatised in one way or another during the following years. Many of their new owners kept the type running well into the twenty-first century with the last of the type making their final journeys on route 159 on 9 December 2005.

The author would like to acknowledge reference to the websites maintained by Ian Armstrong and Ian Smith with regards to the vehicle requirements for London bus routes and information relating to London Transport buses. In each case any data quoted is relevant to the date the image was recorded. My familiarity with London is not as it used to be, and has not been helped by the vast amount of changes that have taken place. However, with the aid of Google Street View, it has proved possible to identify the exact location of where virtually every picture was recorded and, consequently, to contrast today's street scene with that of forty or more years ago. All the photographs included in this book were taken by the author, who retains copyright.

Mike Rhodes
October 2019

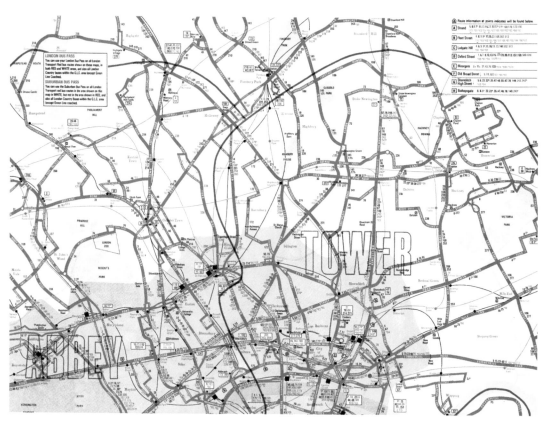

Extract from the London Buses Route Map No. 1 1981.

RM1181 spent almost all of its working life allocated to garages south of the river. In this view it is seen on 21 January 1978 turning round at the Saturday terminus of route 1 in Bromley Road, opposite Catford (TL) garage. On Mon–Fri it operated through to Bromley (TB) garage. The Saturday allocation called for sixteen RMs from New Cross (NX) garage. The route retained RMs until 4 June 1987. Daneby Road is in the background.

Route 1A, running between Willesden (AC) garage and Greenwich, was introduced on 1 January 1967, on Sundays only, with RTs from New Cross garage. It was altered to start from Trafalgar Square from 25 October 1969, then requiring just five RMs. RM647 is seen in Rotherhithe Road, near Surrey Docks (renamed Quays) station, on Sunday 15 October 1978, just two weeks before the service was withdrawn.

To celebrate the Queen's Silver Jubilee London Transport (LT) repainted twenty-five Routemasters in this mainly all-over silver livery. RM1850 has been renumbered to SRM25 and is seen at Golders Green bus station on 18 July 1977. At the time the Mon–Fri allocation was for twenty RMs from Stockwell (SW) garage. This long-standing route was largely replaced by new route 322 from October 1992.

Route 2B originated at Swiss Cottage (North Finchley on Sundays) and passed right through the heart of central London, crossing the Thames by way of Vauxhall Bridge on its way to Crystal Palace. On 16 March 1985, RMs 785 and 1531 are seen with RM1421 on route 3, in Crystal Palace Parade. This arrangement of on-street parking was later replaced by a bus station just to the right of the first RM.

On 7 October 1976, RM1235, from Norwood (N) garage, is seen with RM263 in Crystal Palace Parade. At the time, route 3 was operated by both Norwood and Chalk Farm (CF) garages. RM1235 was an early causality of the 1980s Routemaster cull, being despatched to Booth's of Rotherham for scrap in January 1985. RM263 has a non-opening front window body, which were originally confined to production models RM 5-253 when built.

Route 5 was introduced on 11 November 1959 running from Barking garage (BK) to Bloomsbury with RMs from Poplar (PR) and West Ham (WH) garages. From 17 April 1971 it was converted to operation using 'OPO' DMS vehicles. In April 1981 it was converted back to RM operation and was now running between East Ham White Horse and Waterloo. RM805 is seen in a busy Barking Road at East Ham on 20 March 1982.

Throughout the 1970s Oxford Street, in the heart of the Capital's shopping district, thronged with Routemasters. In fact there were eleven RM-worked routes plying their trade between Marble Arch and Regent Street when this picture was taken on 14 August 1976. Hackney (H) garage's RML2491 is en route from Kensal Rise station to Hackney Wick with RMLs 2483 and 2462 following close behind, the latter also on route 6.

RM674 of Middle Row (X) garage is showing Acton Tram Depot on the ultimate destination blind as it passes the junction of Winchester Street with Acton High Street. It is seen on Friday 25 August 1978, when its starting point would have been Tottenham Court Road station. The depot last saw trams *c*. 1936 and closed the year after but was resurrected by First Uxbridge Buses in 1990, before being closed again several years later.

RML2471 is seen passing the iconic Selfridges store in Oxford Street on 15 July 1978. At this time, route 8 required thirty-nine Routemasters from Willesden (AC) and Bow (BW) garages on a Saturday. By way of a contrast, Red Arrow route 500 had an allocation of just four AEC Merlins from Victoria (GM) garage on this day of the week. MBA566 is waiting patiently behind.

Butterwick bus station, at Hammersmith, sees RM1353 waiting to leave on a route 9 journey from Aldwych to Mortlake (M) garage on 16 July 1977. Although a relatively short route by London standards, it still boasted an allocation of twenty buses on a Saturday. Whilst the area has now somewhat changed with the provision of a new bus station, the building in the left background, known as Welbeck Mansions, was functioning as an Italian restaurant in 2019.

The 9A variant was introduced on 11 April 1971 and ran from Aldgate bus station to Mortlake (M) garage, usually on Sundays only. However, RMs 103 and 1582 are seen at Trafalgar Square, stuck in the mother of all traffic jams, on spring bank holiday Monday 6 June 1977. Whilst RM103 is only going as far as Kensington Palace Gate, RM1582 is attempting to do the full journey. The 9A was absorbed by route 9 in April 1981.

RMs 1938 and 1816 are seen resting at the Hammersmith Brook Green terminus of route 11 on Saturday 16 June 1979. The 11 retained its Routemasters until October 2003 (Sundays excepted), when it was eventually converted to 'OPO' with Wrightbus-bodied Volvos working from Stockwell (SW) garage. The building in the background is Grade II listed and was originally an assembly plant and showroom for Ford's Model T in 1916.

Peckham garage forecourt plays host to RM1910 (SRM11) and RML2265 on Sunday 5 June 1977. Running from Norwood Junction to Harlesden on Mon–Sat, route 12 had an allocation of sixty-four buses from four garages. The Sunday allocation, however, was a more modest nineteen buses when it terminated at Shepherds Bush Green. Peckham (PM) garage was closed in 1994 and later demolished, although the towering wall in the background still survives.

Whitehall was another central London thoroughfare that was well served by Routemasters in the early 1980s. Peckham (PM) garage's RM387 was only going as far as Dulwich Plough on 29 April 1983, whilst RM660 is heading for Hammersmith Broadway on route 11. Standing at 169 feet and 3 inches tall, Nelson's Column has been watching over the London transport scene since 1843.

RML884 was one of the initial batch of twenty-four long Routemasters that entered service in 1961. In this 18 June 1979 view it has just turned off Ballards Lane into Nether Street at the North Finchley terminus of route 13 from Aldwych. Nether Street is now pedestrianised.

It was not unusual to see Routemasters, at wayside locations, with their bonnets up – perhaps cooling down, although RML2631 is seen on 28 October 1979. The location is the Putney terminus of route 14 in Oxford Road, which was situated off Upper Richmond Road. RML2631 continued in service, latterly with London General, until July 2005.

RM1008 is seen in East Ham High Street South approaching the White Horse terminus of route 15 on a sunny but cold 11 February 1978. Routemasters took over from RTW/RTLs in 1964 and remained in charge on Mon–Fri daytime schedules until August 2003. Meanwhile, RM1008 was sold for scrap in October 1986.

Whilst the Sat/Sun allocation was mixed with RMs from Middle Row (X) and RMLs from Upton Park (U), the Mon–Fri allocation on route 15 was for forty-five RMLs from the latter garage when this picture was taken on 21 February 1981. Passengers race to board RML2556 in Oxford Street. By chance this RM is featured three times in the book.

Route 16A was introduced on 31 January 1976 with crewed-DM Fleetlines from Willesden (AC) garage to serve the new Brent Cross Shopping Centre. The DMs were changed for RMLs in May 1980. RMLs 2486, 2405 and 901 are seen on layover at the garage a few weeks later, on 21 June. Now owned by Metroline, the garage site was substantially remodelled in 2009.

Taken on the same day as the picture above, Willesden's RML2608 is waiting to leave Victoria bus station. Had the RMLs not initially been fitted with 'Brent Cross' destination inserts? The service ran through to the Shopping Centre at all times other than in the late evenings. The RMLs remained in charge of the route until November 1987 when Metrobuses took over.

A busy summer's day sees RML2519 making its way along Wembley High Road, passing Wembley Central. When this picture was taken on 27 May 1978, route 18 ran between London Bridge and Sudbury Swan and was operated by Stonebridge Park (SE) garage. The National Westminster Bank has survived the cull of high street branches and was still open for business in 2019. Note the non-standard number blind.

Some of the layover points were quite obscure, as evidenced by this view of RM1724, which is seen at the Tooting Bec terminus of route 19 on 17 June 1979. The location is actually Wheatlands Road, near to the junction of Stapleton Road. By 2018 the bus stand had long since gone and residential parking was the order of the day.

RM1782 is seen descending Eltham Hill on 29 May 1982; the car in the background is emerging from Prince John Road. Route 21 normally ran from Moorgate to Sidcup (SP) garage, although RM1782 is going no further than Lewisham. It was withdrawn from New Cross (NX) garage in April 1994. Meanwhile, the 2019 version of route 21 operated between Newington Green and Lewisham with TfL Wrightbus LT Routemasters.

RM1251 from New Cross (NX) garage is seen at journey's end on a very wet 8 February 1980 – in Finsbury Square at Moorgate. The Square dates back to 1777 and the buildings in the background were originally constructed as town houses. The bus is waiting outside Triton Court, which was developed from 1904–30 and is now the Alphabeta Building.

RM1820 gingerly picks its way along Chatsworth Road as it approaches the 22 terminus in Clifden Road at Homerton on Friday 8 February 1980. The East London Commissions betting shop is now Pack & Clowder (everything for the well-kept dog and cat) whilst the shoe shop is now a hair boutique. Route 22 was cut back to Piccadilly Circus in 1990.

RM1214 and RM241 thread their way through Piccadilly Circus on 16 June 1979, both heading for the southern terminus of route 22 at Putney Common. The London Pavilion Theatre (in the background) opened on 30 November 1885 and closed on 26 April 1981. The first Bond film, *Dr No*, was premiered at this venue, as was the Beatle's film *A Hard Day's Night*. In 2019 route 22 was running between Putney Common and Oxford Circus.

West Ham (WH) garage's RML2550 is on a very short route 23 working having started out at Barking (BK) garage (just visible in the background), and is only going as far as Plaistow. In this 11 February 1978 view it is being pursued by RT3905 along Longbridge Road. Route 87 was the penultimate RT-worked route and was converted to RM operation on 28 October 1978.

Route 24 has run between Hampstead Heath and Pimlico for over 100 years and the scene above could still be replicated in 2019, but the bus would be a Wrightbus TfL LT Routemaster. On 18 June 1979 Chalk Farm (CF) garage's RML2377 was captured laying over at Hampstead Heath. After a brief spell of crewed-Fleetline (DM) operation between October 1975 and April 1979, the allocated type reverted back to traditional Routemasters and remained so until October 1986, when 'OPO' Titans took over.

Quite appropriately, route 25 was the recipient of a handful of silver RMs in 1977. The twenty-five buses were sponsored by individual companies and were allocated to central area routes, being swapped between garages from time to time. RM1871 (SRM7) is seen at Oxford Circus on 4 June 1977 but is only going as far as Ilford Broadway, vice the usual ultimate destination of Becontree Heath.

RM1332 has terminated in Tramway Avenue, round the corner from Stratford Town Hall, on 22 July 1978. At the time the route was shared between West Ham (WH) and Bow (BW) garages, with a combined Saturday allocation of thirty-one buses. Alas, Bill Stevens' Gymnasium is no more.

At the time this picture was taken, route 26 ran from New Barnet station (Chesterfield Road on Sundays) to Golders Green station and employed just four RMs on Mon–Fri from Finchley (FY) garage. RM1708 is seen at the northern terminus on 18 June 1979. From 27 September 1980 it was extended to Brent Cross Shopping Centre using 'OPO' Metrobuses.

Throughout the 1970s the weekend service on route 27 was projected beyond Richmond to Teddington. RMs 138 and 1096, both of Fulwell (FW) garage, are seen on the garage forecourt on early May bank holiday, 5 May 1980. Usually Fulwell only provided buses for the 27 on a Sunday (and presumably bank holidays). However, of more significance is the fact that this was the day when the SAS stormed the Iranian Embassy in London to bring the hostage crisis to an end.

RM979 has not made it as far as Richmond but has terminated at Kew Green. It is seen on 16 July 1977, before starting back towards Archway. It spent its entire LT career of twenty-five years working from four different garages. Initially allocated to Finchley (FY) in October 1961, it moved to Holloway (HT) in November 1973, before seeing out its time at Middle Row and then Westbourne Park (both X). It was sold for scrap in 1986.

Four Routemasters on four different routes are seen at Golders Green station on 27 May 1978. RM2149 will depart for Harlesden on the 260 whilst RM1840 on the 2 is displaying Stockwell. In the distance can be seen newly overhauled RML2430 (originally a London Country bus until bought by LT in December 1977) on a 13 diagram, whilst to the left is RM1112, which is bound for Wandsworth.

Wandsworth (WD) garage's RM428 has only travelled as far north as West Hampstead on route 28 on 21 June 1980. Whilst displaying West End Green, the layover stand was in nearby Hillfield Road. This was another instance of an obscure location for a bus stand. RM428 was later converted to an open-top bus and was last reported as operating for De Zigeuner Tours of Liege, in Belgium, in 2015.

Route 29 ran from Victoria to Enfield and was 13.3 miles in length, employing fifty-two Routemasters from three garages on Mon–Fri. RMs 1063 and 615 are seen at the Enfield Palace Gardens terminus on 19 November 1977. This area was completely redeveloped in the mid-2000s to accommodate the Palace Gardens Shopping Centre.

Between March 1977 and April 1983 Palmers Green (AD) garage's contribution to route 29 on a Sunday was for eight RMs. Recently overhauled, RM529 has stopped for a crew change in Green Lanes, close to the garage, on 18 April 1982. By 2019 the petrol service station in the background (corner of Elmdale Road) had been replaced by a modern low-rise block of flats.

Route 30 remained unchanged for almost twelve years from June 1967, during which time it was operated by Routemasters from Putney (AF) and Hackney (H) garages. Normally running between Hackney Wick and Roehampton, RM1936 is terminating at Marble Arch, where it is seen on 15 July 1978.

Operation of route 31 had flirted between RTLs and RTWs between 1950 and 1965, followed by standard RTs before Routemasters were first introduced on Sundays, in 1969. RMs 1282 and 1263, from Chalk Farm (CF) and Battersea (B) garages respectively, are seen at the Camden Town terminus, in Bayham Street, on 22 July 1978.

RM1432 is seen at the route 31 terminus in Hobury Street, just off the King's Road, at Chelsea World's End, on 16 June 1979. Along with route 28, the 31 was converted to 'OPO' in the spring of 1989 using a fleet of Mercedes-Benz minibuses based at Westbourne Park (X) garage.

Stamford Brook (V) garage was originally built as Chiswick Tram Depot and was later used as a base for the BEA Routemaster-operated services to Heathrow Airport. Following a two-year refit, it was reopened as an LT bus garage in 1980. On the occasion of the open day, 3 July 1983, at nearby Chiswick bus works, RMs 684 and 1439 are seen with visiting Eastbourne Borough Transport Dennis Dominator No. 46.

Stockwell (SW) bus garage was opened in April 1952 and, at the time, was something of a groundbreaking design, with the roof being supported by large-span concrete arches. It was accredited as a Grade II listed building in 1988. Seen beneath the arches, on 10 April 1977, are RMs 533 and 1657 and RML2265, along with a contingent of Scottish coaches with Eastern Scottish XA359 and Alexander Northern NPE34 prominent.

One could be forgiven for assuming this was a scene inside a London Transport garage. However the clue that it isn't is the green Leyland National on the extreme right. This is Southdown's Whitehark garage in Brighton, on Sunday 3 May 1981, on the occasion of the annual Historic Commercial Vehicle Society (HCVS) London to Brighton rally. On the left is former London Country RCL2239, then allocated to Stamford Hill (SF) garage, whilst alongside is RML2474 from Hanwell (HL) and finally RM1186 from Merton (M).

No mistaking this location – a view inside Barking (BK) garage on the morning of the final day of RT operation – 7 April 1979. RT1790, which was new in June 1950, has run its last mile for London Transport and the garage foreman is about to remove the destination blind from above the platform. Meanwhile, newly transferred in from store at Clapham is RM539, which will take up duties on route 62. RMs were short-lived on the 62, with 'OPO' Leyland Titans taking over in September 1982.

Throughout the 1970s the compact Mortlake (M) garage provided Routemasters for routes 9 and 33. RM1633 is seen in Rocks Lane, skirting Barnes Common, on 16 June 1979. Following close behind is London Country Leyland National SNB335, on Greenline route 714, from Baker Street to Dorking.

Old Town, on the edge of Clapham Common, was and still is a focal point for a number of London bus routes. These two Routemasters, seen on 21 July 1978, will depart in different directions as RM1410 will head north to Hackney Wick and RM577 will head directly south along the A24 to Morden. Whilst RM1410 went for scrap in October 1982, RM577 later worked for both Southend Transport and Reading Mainline.

The 36 family of routes were all worked by Routemasters from Peckham (PM) garage during the 1970s. That is until the disastrous MCW Scania Metropolitan (MD) took over in March/April 1976. So unreliable were these buses (with LT) that all three of the 36 group had reverted back to RM operation by the end of 1980. Still officially operated by MDs, RM480 is deputising for an MD and is seen on the bus stand in Vauxhall Bridge Road, on 6 May 1980.

RM1320 is seen reposing at the West Kilburn terminus of route 36B on 5 May 1980. This is another picture taken on the day of the Iranian Embassy siege. In the background is Queen's Park station, whilst the building on the right is now demolished. Route 36 was still using this stand in 2019.

Hounslow bus station is situated adjacent to the bus garage (AV) and was a busy transport hub for many years, accommodating more than a dozen routes. RML2466, of Putney (AF) garage, waits to leave for Brixton on 26 March 1977, whilst RML2616 waits behind. The bus station roof was removed in the mid-2000s.

The route 37 allocation was shared by three garages. New Cross (NX) had joined the fray in October 1975 and in this view, taken on 21 July 1978, NX's RML2716 is seen in The Pavement, going the full distance to Peckham. Manny Harris Ltd is now Images whilst the green in the background is Clapham Common.

Victoria bus station has been depicted many times over the years and is recorded as being London's busiest. For many years without a roof, RM142 is seen under the canopy on 6 May 1980. The roof was later removed in 2003. The 38 was an early recipient of the TfL LT Routemaster, in May 2014, with buses departing for Hackney at up to three-minute intervals. The 38 also flirted with bendi-buses from 2005–09.

Silver Jubilee year again and RM1903 (SRM15) is seen pulling out of Capworth Street on 6 June, as it approaches the Leyton Green terminus. SRM15 moved to Streatham (AK) garage shortly afterwards where it was used on the 159.

This picture typifies some of the obscure locations of London's terminus bus stands of the era. RM44, from Poplar (PR) garage, is seen at rest in Hurst Street, in Herne Hill, on 21 July 1978. The Lambeth Council dust cart would now be a prime candidate for display in a museum.

For a period during the Second World War route 41 was extended beyond Tottenham Hale right through to Dagenham Dock. RM1394 is seen at the southern terminus in MacDonald Road at Archway on 4 November 1978. The route has changed very little over the years and was operated by Wrightbus Gemini VDLs in 2019.

Route 43 lost its Sunday service way back in 1958 and it wasn't reinstated until 1991. For many years the route was worked by Muswell Hill (MH) garage, until it closed in July 1990. At the time this picture was taken, 25 November 1978, it was in the hands of crew-operated Fleetlines (DMs), although some RMs were clearly retained to supplement the DMs, as evidenced by RM2062.

The 45 was a bit of an odd route and crossed the River Thames twice. After leaving South Kensington station, it initially headed south and crossed the river by way of Battersea Bridge Road, before turning east and heading towards Camberwell, from where it proceeded north to Elephant & Castle and then by way of Blackfriars Bridge (over the river for a second time) on its journey to Archway. RM1153 is seen in Battersea Bridge Road, passing the junction of Ethelburga Street, on 3 July 1983.

A summer's evening outside the George & Dragon, in Farnborough, sees RMs 1563 and 342 waiting before their scheduled departures north, with the latter purporting to be going the full distance to Shoreditch. The date is 2 June 1977. Alas, both the pub and the terminus are no more, the hard standing having been landscaped in 1985.

The 47 was (and partly still is) a long north to south route which had a number of intermediate starting and finishing points. In this 8 February 1980 view, RM2081 has terminated at Tooley Street in Southwark and is only going as far south as Catford (TL) garage. The entrance on the right, beyond the phone box, is Weaver's Lane whilst St John's Tavern has been converted to offices. The building on the left has been refurbished but, alas, the tree has been felled.

The northern terminus of route 48 from London Bridge was both inhospitable and unwelcoming, being situated near the busy Whipps Cross roundabout where Whipps Cross Road meets Lea Bridge Road. Former London Country RML2332 is waiting to leave the stand on a short working to Dalston, on 22 July 1978.

Route 49 had a Mon–Fri allocation of thirty-two Routemasters split between Streatham (AK) and Merton (AL) garages. Merton's RM1705 was caught on 2 June 1977 passing Tooting Bec station, heading north to Shepherds Bush. RMs continued on the 49 for another ten years until 'OPO' Metrobuses took over. The Midland Bank is now a doctor's surgery.

The stand at Farnborough also played host to route 51 until it was replaced by the 229, in May 1977. In fact, Routemasters only worked the 51 for eleven months, bridging the gap between RT and DMS operation. RMs 34 and 786, on the 51, keep RM401, on the 47, company on 9 April 1977. Both 51s will make the long journey back to Woolwich, via Orpington, Sidcup and Plumstead.

Route 52's allocation of buses remained stable throughout the whole of the 1970s, requiring thirteen RMs from Willesden (AC) and five from Middle Row (X) on Sundays. RM1997, from Willesden garage, is seen at Victoria on 26 July 1981, just three weeks before that garage's involvement on a Sunday ended (although it was reintroduced twelve months later).

Two RMs on route 53 are seen proceeding down Whitehall on 29 April 1983, but are heading for different destinations. Whilst RM531 is going the full distance to Plumstead, RM118 is only going as far as New Cross (NX) garage, its home base. Field Marshal Prince George (1819–1904), Duke of Cambridge, pays no heed to the passing traffic. Route 53 had also been blighted by the Scania Metropolitans between 1977 and 1981.

RM1350 has stopped in Croydon Road, in Elmers End, to set down an elderly couple on a bright and crisp Friday 10 March 1978. Route 54 had remained RT-operated from Croydon (TC) garage on Mon–Fri until 22 April 1978, with 'OPO' Fleetlines taking over from that date, so the RM would appear to be deputising for a Regent.

This version of route 55 had an intriguing history over a short period of time. Introduced in October 1969 with RTs from Leyton (T) garage, it initially ran from Walthamstow (WW) garage to Marylebone station. 'OPO' Fleetlines (DMSs) took over in October 1972, whilst the ultimate destination changed to Aldwych in April 1978. Routemasters then took over in January 1981 when the route was extended to Victoria. RM1888 is seen at Walthamstow Central station on 19 April 1982.

Whatever the word is for a group of Routemasters it must surely apply here as four members of the class are seen together at the Crooked Billet terminus of route 58. The Saturday allocation of twenty-four buses was shared between West Ham (WH) and Walthamstow (WW) garages. RMs 809, 2137, 422 and 927 are pictured on 4 June 1977.

Route 59 had been a Sundays-only route since 1948, running initially between West Hampstead and Chipstead Valley. In 1970 the southern destination was altered to Old Coulsdon. In the latter half of 1978 a day Red Bus Rover ticket cost £1.20 and for that princely sum the traveller could enjoy a 21-mile ride on the same bus. RM863 is nearing journey's end and is seen climbing Mead Way at Coulsdon on 15 October 1978, just two weeks before the route was withdrawn.

A busy scene, captured in Longbridge Road, in Barking. The date is Saturday 7 April 1979 – the last day of RT operation with London Transport. During the morning, several of the RT duties were swapped over to RM operation, leaving just RT624 in service for the final journey. RM377 has just replaced RT2541 on the 62 and the garage foreman is about to take the latter into the garage.

A number of Routemasters gained celebrity status and were cared for by dedicated garage staff whilst still remaining in service with LT. One such bus was RM1000. Sporting a unique registration marque (100BXL), RM1000 entered service from West Ham (WH) garage in March 1962, and was withdrawn from Croydon (TC) in June 1985. In June 1983 it attended a prestigious bus rally in Cardiff and is seen outside the Welsh capital's City Hall on Sunday the 26th.

In 1979 sixteen Routemasters were painted in this garish colour scheme to operate a shopper's service around the West End stores. Politically motivated, the venture was not a success and was short-lived. Operated out of Stockwell (SW) garage, RMs 2159 and 2146 are seen laying over in Park Lane, near Marble Arch, on 16 June. The phone boxes are now painted red.

Not a passing glance from the soldiers of the Household Cavalry as they pass the line of silver Routemasters, all lined up to celebrate Her Majesty's twenty-five years on the throne. SRM16 (RM1920) was sponsored by Kleenex and worked on route 19. It is seen in South Carriage Drive on 10 April 1977.

A number of garages had a 'Showbus' amongst their ranks – a bus which was cared for by members of the garage fraternity and kept in pristine condition. RM704 from Sidcup garage (SP) has Brighton's Regency architecture as a backdrop as it proceeds along the town's (at the time) Marine Parade on a day trip to the seaside, on Sunday 4 May 1980 – the occasion of the annual London to Brighton HCVS rally.

Route 63 was another unfortunate service which was inflicted with the Scania Metropolitans, the type being allocated to the route from September 1976 for six years. Either side of this period RMs were in charge. RM1104 is seen at Crystal Palace Parade, setting off back for King's Cross, on 16 March 1985. Later in the year the route was converted to 'OPO' with Leyland Titans.

Ealing Broadway (vice Argyle Road) became the main northern terminus for route 65 in November 1968, and at the same time the route was cut back from Leatherhead (LH) garage to Chessington Zoo. RTs continued to be employed on the route until October 1975, when RMs took over. In this picture, taken on 9 October 1976, RM1649 seems to be in spot of bother whilst RM2033 waits to depart.

RM1043 is seen in Petersham Road in Richmond on 16 July 1977. Through the trees can be seen the bridge which carries Bridge Street over the River Thames. The gap is now occupied by a new building known as Richmond Place, whilst Alpine Fires is now Pier 1 Fish & Chips. Nearly two years later, route 65 would be greatly affected by a road subsidence in this locality, which was infamously referred to as the 'Petersham Hole'.

Chessington Zoo (now known as Chessington World of Adventures) continued to be the southern terminus of route 65 on a daily basis until February 1987, when the route was cut back to Kingston on Mon–Sat. RMs had remained in control until February 1986. RMs 1043 and 2030 are seen at journey's end on 16 July 1977, with the latter still sporting gold London Transport fleet names and numbers.

Although the southern terminus of route 68 was South Croydon (TC) garage, these four Routemasters are seen laying over alongside Brighton Road (actually in High Street), at Purley. The vehicle allocation on Mon–Fri was for forty-seven RMs from three garages. RMs 812, 2197, 1401 and 1392 are seen on Friday 10 March 1978.

RM2071 has called in at West Croydon bus station on its long journey north to Chalk Farm (CF), its home garage. Alongside is RT840, which is only going as far as Catford (CT) garage – again its home base. At this time, 31 January 1977, the 75 only had one more month of RT operation (RM on a Sunday) before 'OPO' Fleetlines (DMS) took over. The old West Croydon bus station has long since vanished.

RM2211, from Croydon (TC) garage, is seen calling in at Euston station on 4 May 1981. Route 68 has largely survived the passage of time and was still plying its trade between Euston and West Norwood in 2019, being operated by the modern-day LT Routemaster type. Sadly RM2211 was sold for scrap in July 1987. The building to the right (East Lodge) was part of the original Euston station (along with the West Lodge), both of which now function as the Euston Tap pub.

The River Thames did not particularly present an obstacle to foot travellers, as North Woolwich could be reached from the East End via routes 69 and 101; a short hop on the Woolwich Free Ferry across the river would present further bus opportunities to continue your journey south. RMs 28 and 956 are seen at the North Woolwich terminus on Saturday 11 February 1978.

RM13 was newly transferred into West Ham (WH) garage from Hackney (H), when this picture was taken at Walthamstow Central on 26 October 1979. The route was shared with Walthamstow (WW) garage and had a peak requirement of thirty-three buses on Mon–Fri. This picture depicts some of the gloomiest weather encountered by the author in the pursuit of the Routemaster.

Route 71 was similarly affected by the 'Petersham Hole', which infamously closed the A307 for sixteen months, from May 1979. Consequently, route 71 only worked as far as Petersham, with passengers transferring on foot around the obstruction to board a 65 for the remainder of the journey to Richmond. RM1991 is seen alongside St Andrew's Church, in Maple Road, in Surbiton, on 9 February 1980. Cost of repairs was over £2.2m.

Riverside (R) garage was responsible for the operation of route 72, which had an allocation of just seven buses Sat/Sun. The East Acton terminus was usually shown as Du Cane Road on the blind, although RM815 is waiting in the adjacent Old Oak Common Lane on 16 June 1979. The driver takes a quick cigarette break before setting off back to Roehampton.

Tottenham (AR) garage supplied thirty-six Routemasters to work the frequent 73 route on a Saturday (fifty-nine on Mon–Fri). In this autumnal 21 October 1978 scene, five RMs can be seen at Stoke Newington Common (with a further three just out of sight). Those on view are numbers 1823, 1397, 1437, 1027 and 1853. They were all scrapped in the 1980s, except for RM1397, which survived into preservation.

RMs 2141 and 1906, both on route 6, hold back at Piccadilly Circus to let RM1704 through the traffic congestion on 26 July 1981. At the time, Twickenham station was only reached on a Sunday, with Hounslow being the ultimate destination on Mon–Sat. Front windows are down on all three buses, so it must have been a warm day.

RM1832 is seen on bank holiday Monday, 5 May 1980, at the normally Sunday-only terminus of Twickenham station. This stop was still occasionally used in 2018 by Transport for London LT Routemasters turning short on route 267. Also, the small brick building on the right still survives.

Route 74 enjoyed a stable sixteen years of operation when Routemasters took over from RTWs in November 1965. RML2563 is seen in Greenland Road, at the junction of Bayham Street in Camden Town, on 22 July 1978. This being a Saturday, the journey to Putney Heath was scheduled to take fifty-one minutes.

The Mon–Fri-only 74B was introduced on 14 August 1963 with RTWs from Riverside (R) garage. Routemasters took over in November 1965 and the allocation of twelve buses remained constant, until the route was withdrawn, after Friday 27 October 1978. RML2646 is seen departing Hammersmith Broadway, on a short working to Baker Street station, on the very last day the route operated.

In 1969 route 76 had played host both to the front-entrance Routemaster, FRM1 (see page 95), and the Atlantean type (XA). At the time this picture was taken, on Saturday 22 July 1978, it ran between Mansion House station and Tottenham (AR) garage with an allocation of just eight RMs. RM426 is seen in Stamford Hill, near the junction of Amhurst Park.

Following the silver RMs and the red and yellow Shop Linkers, LT's next deviation from the norm was to paint fourteen RMs in this commemorative 'Shillibeer' livery to celebrate 150 years since the introduction of the omnibus in London. Twelve RMs from Merton (AL) garage were deployed on the 77 on a Saturday. In a scene that remains largely unchanged today, RM2191 is seen in Millbank, at Westminster, on 16 June 1979.

Almost exactly a year later, on 21 June 1980, RM130 is seen emerging from The Strand at Trafalgar Square. On Saturdays the 77 started from Aldwych, vice Euston station, on Mon–Fri. Tooting Mitre was the final destination, whereas during the week it penetrated as far south as Wallington.

The 77 group of routes was fairly closely linked and, whilst the 77 served Tooting, the 77A/C both served Raynes Park. Meanwhile, the 77B route number was disused between May 1973 and April 1981, when it was reintroduced on Sundays only between Clapham Junction and Raynes Park. RM654 is seen on a 77A journey at Euston station on 29 April 1983. It was withdrawn from service just a year later.

RM462 is seen at journey's end, alongside Raynes Park station, on 9 February 1980. The stand was shared at the time with routes 157 and M1, the latter being a local flat-fare route based on Morden, which had been introduced in March 1969 with AEC Merlins (MBS). The 77C was withdrawn in April of the following year.

Routemasters had been introduced to route 83 as early as December 1966 and the route had been solely in the hands of Alperton (ON) garage since November 1958. The progress of RM2130 is checked by an inspector outside Alperton station on 27 May 1978. RM2130 was painted in 'Shillibeer' livery the following year and worked out of Norbiton (NB) garage on route 65. It was withdrawn and scrapped in 1987.

Golders Green bus station is the setting for this portrait of RM648 and RML2296, which were captured together on 3 May 1980. Route 83 required twenty-one buses to run the service on a Saturday. The Sunday allocation had been in the hands of 'OPO' buses since May 1971 but the Mon–Sat requirement did not follow suit until September 1982.

When first introduced in 1959, there was a four-garage involvement with the operation of route 86, which initially ran between Limehouse and Upminster. It was cut back to Romford station in the east in July 1970, by which time only two garages contributed buses. Upton Park's (U) RML2556 is seen in Ilford High Road, at the junction of Cranbrook Road, on 9 April 1977.

In a largely unchanged scene (the British Railways sign no longer adorns the bridge) RM1712 is seen in Romford South Street on 10 February 1980. Route 87 was the penultimate RT-operated route with RMs taking over on 28 October 1978. Principally worked by Barking (BK) garage, Romford (NS) had a small involvement on a Sunday. RM1712 was sold for scrap in September 1984.

The 87 was worked in two overlapping sections: Harold Hill Gooshays Drive to Barking Blakes Corner and Becontree Heath to Rainham Abbey Wood Lane. In the 1970s the latter still presented a somewhat rural atmosphere, as evidenced by this picture of RM535, which is seen at the Wood Lane terminus on 26 October 1979. Houses now occupy the open space on the left.

Mitcham Cricketers was a familiar destination shown by buses working on route 88 and became the ultimate destination in January 1974. RMLs 2643 and 2261 are seen alongside the green in London Road on 3 March 1984. Alas, the Cricketers PH (which stood just to the left) was closed in August 2010 and has now been demolished. MCW Metrobus M955 is seen behind on the 44.

If you wanted to see Routemasters in any numbers then Oxford Street was the place to visit. RML2749 is displaying 'Mitcham Cricketers' in its rear ultimate destination box as it heads east along Oxford Street, towards Oxford Circus, on 21 February 1981. It would take it another hour or so to reach its final destination. Twenty-four RMLs were scheduled for the route from Shepherds Bush (S) and Stockwell (SW) garages on a Saturday.

During the period covered by this book London Transport held two open days at their vast Aldenham Bus Overhaul Works. The first of these was on 16 September 1979. An unidentified RM body is seen suspended in mid-air. The chassis and bodies were overhauled separately. This body will be married up with a finished chassis and will take the fleet number that was assigned to the vehicle/chassis registration number.

The second such event was held on 25 September 1983 and newly overhauled RML2556 is seen on the tilt test apparatus. The unladen bus must demonstrate its stability and will pass its test if it sustains an angle of 28 degrees from the vertical position with all four wheels remaining on the base plate. RML2556 is still unsupported at 33 degrees.

An unidentified RML is seen in the paint shop area on 16 September 1979. The window glass, lights and radiator have all been masked out and the remainder of the bodywork sprayed LT Mail Red. The mudguards have been painted black and the white band has been applied. It will not be long before this bus is back on the road.

RM1318 (the number is shown marked on the windscreen) is seen on one of the invertors which enable the bus body to be turned almost on its side so that the underside can be made more easily accessible. Aldenham Works was opened in 1956 and closed in November 1986. The building was eventually demolished in July 1996 and the site is now occupied by the Centennial Park business park.

It is Sunday 28 October 1979 and RM521 has been captured in the early morning gloom in Priory Road, at North Cheam. On this day of the week route 93 commanded an allocation of ten Routemasters from Sutton (A) garage. Converted to 'OPO' in April 1983, it was still running between the same two points in 2019.

Route 93 again and RM425 is seen in London Road, at Morden, on Friday 21 July 1978. The Mon–Fri vehicle requirement was twice the Sunday allocation. RM425 only saw service from one more garage, Holloway (HT), before it was withdrawn in May 1985, when it was sold for scrap. The Art Wallpapers shop is long gone and the building is now a Relate charity shop.

Route 94 only had a four-year stint of Routemaster operation. It was the last route south of the Thames to retain its RTs, these giving way to RMs on 28 October 1978. The route was withdrawn altogether in September 1982 when it was replaced by new routes 208 and 261. RM2056 is seen in Bromley High Street on 27 October 1979.

RM2140 waits in the lay-by in Bromley Common, at the junction of Johnson Road, on 29 May 1982. London Country's ten-year-old MCW-bodied Leyland PDR1A/1 No. AN120, from Godstone (GD) garage (which was closed in 1990), saunters past on route 410 to Biggin Hill Valley. RM2140 was another Routemaster that didn't survive the mid-1980s cull. Towering in the background is the spire of St Luke's Church.

The area of Bishopgate, around Liverpool Street station, has changed dramatically since this picture of RM310 was taken on 26 May 1978. Indeed the route itself didn't survive for much longer, being withdrawn in October of that year. The Great Eastern Trading Co. (household electrical shop) clearly takes its name from the adjacent GE Railway which was formed in 1862, with Liverpool Street becoming the company's terminus in 1874.

The last Routemaster, numerically, RML2760 is seen at the White Horse (PH now demolished) bus stop in East Ham, with a northbound journey on route 101 to Wanstead Flats on 11 February 1978. RML2760 was allocated to Upton Park (U) garage from 1975 until 2003 and passed into preservation in 2005. Route 101 was converted to crewed-Fleetline (DM) operation three months after this picture was taken.

RML2548 is seen under a threatening sky, crossing the double-bascule road bridge (dating from 1920) at the head of the Royal Albert Dock, as it approaches the North Woolwich terminus of route 101, on 9 April 1977. The dock no longer plays host to commercial shipping and the bridge has been replaced by a much more modern structure. Even route 101 no longer serves North Woolwich, having been diverted to terminate at Gallions Reach Shopping Park in 2008.

RT-type buses were first introduced to the 102 in October 1949 and remained associated with the route until February 1978, when the Mon–Fri service finally succumbed to the Routemaster. The Saturday allocation was for six RMs from Palmers Green (AD) garage and five RMLs from Muswell Hill (MH). The mixed allocation is depicted at Golders Green, on 27 May 1978, with RM1327 and RML2289.

Route 104 was introduced on 8 November 1961 as part of stage 12 of the trolleybus conversion programme, thereafter replacing the 609 running between the same two points, Barnet and Moorgate. It was cut back to North Finchley in January 1971. RMLs 2509 and 2373 are seen in Finsbury Square, at Moorgate, on 8 February 1980.

RML2572, from Holloway (HT) garage, is seen at the North Finchley terminus of route 104 on 18 June 1979; the location is Nether Street. The route was withdrawn in its entirety in August 1985. Regrettably, it is also no longer possible to consume a refreshing pint in the corner pub (Cricketers, dating from 1881), as the building is now known as Kidz Escape.

Southall's (HW) fairly pristine-looking RM1784 is seen taking a breather, on 27 May 1978, outside Shepherd's Bush (S) garage, the eastern terminus of route 105 from Heathrow Airport. RTs had only finished on the route a month beforehand. Although RM1784 is only going as far as Southall, the full journey was scheduled to take around seventy minutes.

Back in 1979 the building on the left was offering the services of a Public Weighbridge. Regrettably, this intriguing-looking structure has been demolished and the site is now occupied by the Poplar Royal Mail Depot. Having been worked by 'OPO' Fleetlines from August 1972, RMs were reintroduced to the 106 in March 1979. RM26 is seen in Burdett Road, at Limehouse, seven months later, on 27 October.

The frightening aspect of this picture is that, whilst the iconic Routemaster remains unchanged in its appearance to this day, the young child in the pram will now be in his forties. RM1116 is seen making its way along London Road, in the vicinity of West Croydon station, on 25 August 1978.

Route 109 was first introduced in April 1951 as a tramway replacement route running from Victoria Embankment to Purley and the route remained largely unchanged until 1998, when it was cut back to Croydon. At one stage, in 1976, there were four different types of bus allocated to the route at the same time, with RT/RMs on Mon–Fri, DM/RTs on Saturday and DMSs on Sunday. RM1401 is seen at journey's end in Brighton Road, at Purley, on 10 March 1978.

This evocative scene was captured in Wellington Road at St John's Wood on 15 July 1978. Preserved Ribble Motor Services' low-height Leyland PD2/3 No. 1349 (laden with bicycles) has stopped for a breather, while RML2522 heads south on its way from Edgware to Oxford Circus. The PD2 was the support vehicle for a sponsored cycle ride from Preston to Marble Arch (via the A6) and is seen on its return trip north. The location is the junction of Wellington Place.

Route 113 had been exclusively worked by Hendon (AE) garage since October 1939. RML2676 is seen at the Oxford Circus terminus, in John Prince's Street, on 16 June 1979. The type was changed from RM to RMLs in February 1976. Having been converted to 'OPO' in October 1986, it was still running between Oxford Circus and Edgware in 2019 but from Edgware (EW) garage, with Hendon having closed in June 1987.

British European Airways ordered sixty-five Routemasters, which were delivered in 1966/7. They were designed to pull small luggage trailers between its book-in terminal and the airport. NMY 644E is seen at Heathrow Airport on 23 April 1978. By now, already having been reduced in number, the last of the type passed to London Transport in 1979, with this one becoming RMA55. It passed to Blue Triangle in 1998 after having seen use as a Trainer at Shepherd's Bush (S) and Fulwell (FW) garages.

RMC1499 was first allocated to London Country's Epping (EP) garage in October 1962, for service on Greenline routes 718/20/20A. Over the following sixteen years it moved about considerably and was painted in NBC green in 1977. It passed to LT in June 1979 and was later painted red. It is seen negotiating Sloane Square on 6 May 1980. The building to the right is now Tiffany & Co. jewellers.

The full complement of twenty-five silver Routemasters was assembled in South Carriage Drive, alongside Hyde Park, on 10 April 1977 for their official launch into service. Seen here are SRM7 (RM1871), SRM10 (RM1914) and SRM19 (RM1904). The buses assumed their original identities at the end of the year.

Chaos at Victoria – buses jostle for position to exit the bus station. Whilst an RM can be seen in the distance on the 2B, green RCL Trainer No. 2248 is waiting patiently behind. To the left is an AEC Merlin with RMs 142 and 1137 following. Finally another Merlin, MBA547, has just crept into view. The picture was taken on Tuesday 6 May 1980.

From July 1975 route 117 ran daily between Shepherds Bush Green and Staines. The terminus in Staines was in Bridge Street, which was originally the approach to Staines West railway station (which was closed on 29 March 1965). Whilst all traces of the railway and road have now gone, the original station frontage building still stands (out of view on the left). RM1035, from Hounslow (AV) garage, is seen with Kingston's venerable AEC Regal IV RF489 on 4 December 1976.

RM806 is seen in Aberconway Road, in Morden, approaching journey's end from Clapham Common, on 21 July 1978. Route 118 was jointly worked by RMs and RTs for three years from May 1973. R. B. Dreifuss Ltd, the chemists, was acquired by F. Moss in 1994 but is now the Café La Lavella.

From October 1970 route 119 was altered to run on Mon–Fri only, with the Saturday and Sunday services taking the numbers 119A and 119B, respectively. Operated by Bromley (TB) garage, RM295 is seen about to turn from Hayes Lane into Pickhurst Lane, at Hayes, on 1 June 1977 (Epsom Derby Day). On Sat/Sun the service was extended to Thornton Heath.

The Saturday variant of the 119 is seen on the last day of operation, 21 October 1978. From the following weekend the 119A was replaced by the 119 but the Sunday variant, the 119B, was not subsumed until April 1985. RM1116 is seen in Bromley High Street on a short working to Hayes. The occasional RT (94 route allocation) could still be found on the 119/A until they were ousted from Bromley garage a week after the above date.

Bus stations come and go. The 'new' Lewisham bus station was opened on 22 April 1978, which is where RMs 167 and 2032 could be seen on 27 October 1979. The former has worked a route 122 journey from Bexleyheath (BX) garage (although the route was operated by Plumstead). This site was closed on 28 February 2014 for redevelopment and has since been replaced by a new facility close to the railway station.

RM111 is seen in a bustling Powis Street, in the centre of Woolwich, on 18 August 1979. By 2019 Powis Street had been semi-pedestrianised, although the 122 was still running between Crystal Palace and Plumstead with Alexander Dennis Enviro400 Hybrid buses.

Route 135 had absorbed the 135A in August 1977 and was then converted from RT to RM operation five months later. Somewhat of a short route, local to the Enfield area, it required eight buses on Mon–Fri. RM1906 is seen at the Carterhatch terminus on 18 June 1979. The Enfield Council Depot has since been replaced by housing development.

Oops! Just what the driver of this Daimler was thinking as he pulled out into Park Lane is anybody's guess. On 15 July 1978, RM2022 had its journey to Crystal Palace prematurely curtailed by an errant driver. It is likely that RM2022 has started its journey at Oxford Circus; if so it hasn't travelled very far.

The 140 was a lengthy route that ran from Mill Hill Broadway, in the north, via Harrow-on-the-Hill, Yeading and Hayes to Heathrow Airport in the west. It was principally operated by Harrow Weald (HD) garage and had retained RTs through to July 1978. RMs 965 and 65 take time out at the UK's busiest airport on 29 October 1982.

RM628 was found resting in a nondescript location on 9 December 1978, as it takes a breather from the rigours of route 140. The location is Blyth Road, which is close to Hayes & Harlington station. The small building alongside is now Audrey's Hair Salon (not of *Coronation Street* fame).

This was the scene in Bromley Common, opposite Bromley (TB) garage, early on Sunday morning, 30 January 1977. Routemasters were scheduled to operate route 146 on Sundays only (RTs Mon–Sat) from January 1975, until the route was converted to 'OPO' with Bristol LHS midi-buses from 22 April 1978. The allocation was for just one bus, which on this date was RM308. Behind are RMs 342 and 1563, about to start their day's work.

Route 149 was a replacement for trolleybus service 649 running between Waltham Cross and Liverpool Street, but extended to Victoria. When RM652 was captured at Edmonton Green, on 27 August 1983, the route started from Ponders End and was actually scheduled for operation with former London Country RCLs. Liverpool Street was the Sat/Sun southern terminus.

London Country received forty-three enhanced versions of the Routemaster in 1965, which were classified as RCLs. They initially displaced RTs on Greenline services from Romford (RE), Grays (GY) and Hertford (HG) garages. Looking somewhat rundown and now confined to ordinary bus work from Godstone (GD) garage, RCL2222 is seen in Belmont Road at Wallington on 10 March 1978. This bus passed to London Transport in June 1979 and worked from Stamford Hill (SF) garage on the 149.

The RMC was also a coach-seated version of the RM, produced in 1962 and which was initially used to replace the aging Regal RFs on a number of Greenline services. There were sixty-nine of the sub-class numbered CRL(RMC)4 and RMC1453 to 1520. These too were demoted to ordinary bus work before the large majority passed to London Transport. RMC1464 is seen alongside Epsom Racecourse on Derby Day – 1 June 1977.

Exactly 100 of the long Routemasters were allocated to the Country Division (in two batches) when new and these were painted in the green and yellow colours. Eight years after London Country passed to the National Bus Company (NBC), RML2314, seen in Croydon High Street on 10 March 1978, is still sporting the old colours. Fitted with fully automatic gears, they were first introduced to routes 409/10/11 in October 1965.

RML2456 was one of the 1966 batch of fifty Routemasters allocated to the Country Division and was originally based in the north at Harlow (HA) garage. It was transferred to Staines (ST) in October 1972 and is seen in Kingston Road at Staines on 4 December 1976. RML2456 passed to London Transport in 1979 and was later refurbished.

Although allocated to Swanley (SJ) garage, RMC1485 is seen resting outside Dartford's Priory Road (DT) garage on 13 January 1979. The garage was demolished in 1986 and is now the site of a DIY Superstore. RMC1485 also passed to London Transport and was later used on the X15 commuter service from Upton Park (U) garage.

A deserted London Road at Northfleet, on a crisp Saturday morning of 13 January 1979, sees RML2338 heading for Dartford (Joyce Green) on service 480 from Erith. RML2338 never received NBC colours and passed to LT later that year. Remaining in service in the central area until 2002, it is now preserved.

Routemasters were only scheduled to operate on route 150 from February 1976 until October 1977, bridging the gap between RT and 'OPO' Fleetline (DMS) operation. RM1428 is seen turning out of Cranbrook Road into Beal Road, at Ilford, on 9 April 1977. The well-known Moss Bros brand shop is now a mobile phone outlet. Route 150 was withdrawn in June 1986 but the RM survived for another twenty years.

As can be gathered from the sparse intermediate blind display and lack of an ultimate destination, route 151 was somewhat of a short route. In fact, the route from Lewisham to Kidbrooke was only just over 2 miles long and employed just two buses on Mon–Sat. RM1807 is seen in Molesworth Street, in Lewisham, on the last day of Routemaster operation, 21 April 1978. Behind is RM519, laying over on the 21 to Moorgate.

Route 155 from Wimbledon normally terminated at the Elephant & Castle, other than at peak times when it crossed the Thames via Westminster Bridge, ran along Victoria Embankment and then crossed back over Blackfriars Bridge (and vice versa). Viewed from Waterloo Bridge, RM290 is seen on the Embankment on 10 March 1978.

RM1899 is seen crossing what is probably the most famous zebra crossing in the country – situated in Abbey Road in South Hampstead. The Beatles' Abbey Road studio is just behind the bus on the left. The picture was taken on Saturday 27 May 1978, when the service required thirty-four RMs from Streatham (AK) and Camberwell (Q) garages. This was the very last RM-worked route in London (excepting Heritage services).

The West End Green terminus was first used by buses on route 159 in November 1947 and continued as such until March 1992, when the route was cut back to Baker Street station. RMs 614 and 1899 are seen at West Hampstead on 21 June 1980. Parking buses with the entrance facing towards the roadway was a common LT practice.

The leafy terminus at Chislehurst War Memorial was the author's favourite on the whole of the LT system and played host to buses on routes 161 and 161A. The 161 had continued to be worked by RTs on Mon–Sat until 21 May 1977, when RMs took over. Routemasters retained a presence until February 1985, when the route was converted to 'OPO' with Leyland Titans. RM774 is seen on 27 October 1979.

Route 161A followed the same route as the 161 from Woolwich to Chislehurst and then continued on to Petts Wood station. However, whilst the 161 was worked by Sidcup (SP) garage, Abbey Wood (AW) provided the allocation for the 161A. Fresh out of Aldenham Works, RM707 is seen in Well Hall Road, crossing Eltham High Street heading back home on 4 June 1977.

RM1093 is seen in Chislehurst High Street, passing the pond, on Saturday 21 January 1978. The allocation on this day of the week was for ten buses. The 161A number disappeared in September 1980 when all journeys were henceforth numbered 161 with a split allocation from both Sidcup (SP) and Abbey Wood (AW). The latter allocation was transferred to the new Plumstead (PD) garage from October 1981 but using Scania Metropolitans.

Another pair of routes that were closely linked was the 164 and 164A, both of which headed south from Morden station and didn't part company until Banstead. RM1644 is seen in Aberconway Road (passing the junction of Abbotsbury Road), in Morden, on 21 July 1978, having travelled north from Epsom.

Sutton (A) garage was responsible for the allocation of buses on the 164/A with RM429 seen at Tattenham Corner, the southern terminus of route 164A. In the background is Epsom Racecourse, where the Derby classic has been run since 1780. The date is 30 March 1979, which was the last day of operation of route 164A, with the location being served by the DMS-operated route 280A from the following day.

Route 171 ran from Tottenham Bruce Grove to Forest Hill and was associated with the RM for many years, taking over from RT/RTLs in March 1968. This actual layover is in Woodside Gardens (off Bruce Grove), where RM1264 was pictured on 3 May 1980. A look on Google Street View reveals that both the bus stand and the mattress have gone.

Routemasters pass on route 172 in Whitehall. RM139, still with an original-style body, is seen on 29 April 1983 and will have started its journey at King's Cross. By this date the route only operated on Mon–Fri and required thirteen buses from Camberwell (Q) garage. RM139 went for scrap when the route was withdrawn in August 1985. Soldiers of the Household Cavalry can just be seen on the left, at the entrance to Horse Guards Parade.

RM272 is seen in Romford South Street on route 174 on 3 April 1976, closely followed by RT2467 on the convoluted 87 Worked exclusively by Romford (NS) garage, the 174 required twenty RMs on a Saturday for the run from Noak Hill to Dagenham. The UK's railways were still under the jurisdiction of British Railways at the time as proclaimed on the side of the overbridge.

The 175 played host to four different types of bus in a short period of time. Still operated by RTs in the early 1970s, 'OPO' Fleetlines were introduced on Sundays from November 1972. Then, from October 1975, the route was operated by former BOAC Routemasters (RMAs), which had no destination apertures. These were short-lived, and conventional RMs took over in September 1976. RM1567 is seen in Romford South Street on 11 February 1978.

The 176A was introduced on 7 October 1951 as a tramway replacement route and was operated solely by Walworth (WL) garage throughout its entire existence; the vehicle allocation was shared with the 176. RM1272 is seen passing Camberwell Green on 21 July 1978. The route was withdrawn in September 1982.

Operation of route 180 was split evenly between Abbey Wood (AW) and Catford (TL – Tilling Lewisham) garages with no service provided on a Sunday. RM915 is seen passing its home garage in Bromley Road, at Catford, on 10 March 1978. Opened in 1914 by the LGOC, its allocation in 1976 totalled 148 buses, made up of types RT, RM and DMS, of which examples of each could still be found there two years later. The garage was still functioning in 2019 under the aegis of Stagecoach London.

RM1147 has reached South Harrow station and is seen turning into South Hill Avenue on 27 May 1978. Only six RMs from Stonebridge Park (SE) garage were required to operate the service on a Saturday. Following a visit to Aldenham Works a few months later, RM1147 was reallocated to Holloway (HT). It was sold for scrap in October 1988.

Another visit was paid to Mead Way, at Old Coulsdon, (see page 40) on Friday 10 March 1978, where this time, buses on the weekday 190 were observed climbing the hill. Croydon (TC) garage's RM1751 is seen slogging its way up the gradient as it nears the terminus outside The Tudor Rose public house (still standing) in Coulsdon Road. The route was operated by Leyland PD3s, borrowed from Southend Transport (see inset – No. 342 outside West Croydon station), in 1975 due to a shortage of serviceable Routemasters.

The sun has burst through after a heavy shower at Blackheath Village and illuminated a soaking-wet RM1070 as it heads for Plumstead Woodlands Estate. A fairly modest route with a running time of around forty minutes, only eight RMs from New Cross (NX) garage were required to maintain route 192. It is seen passing the Railway public house (on the right), which was still open for business in 2019.

Another miserable day in the Capital and RM490 is seen in Station Lane, at Hornchurch, on 26 October 1979. The route was considerably shortened in September 1982 when it was cut back to Romford, vice Barking, and the vehicle requirement was slashed from eight RMs to three Leyland Titans. Shear Elegance Fashions had become Le Moulin Creperie by 2019. Note the chap behind the bus lowering his shop awning.

When this picture was taken, on 21 July 1978, route 196 had by then become a shadow of its former self. Throughout the 1960s the requirement had been for thirty-three buses on Mon–Fri. RM1650 was one of seven buses required to operate a somewhat truncated version of the route from January 1974, and is seen in Stockwell Park Walk at Brixton. RM1650 was sold to Blackpool Transport in April 1986.

Route 207 commenced running on 9 November 1960 and was a direct replacement for trolleybus route 607. Running the length of the A4020 between Shepherds Bush Green and Uxbridge, the Saturday allocation was for forty-five Routemasters when this picture of RML2554 was captured near Uxbridge station (Bakers Road), on 21 February 1981. At this time the route was scheduled for operation with crewed-Fleetlines (DMs) but these had been entirely ousted by September of the following year.

RM604 is seen in Green Lane, passing Chislehurst Pond, on 21 January 1978. Route 228 was operated by a mixture of types throughout the 1970s. The Mon–Sat allocation had been for RTs, with AEC Merlins (MB) on a Sunday. The Sunday-type allocation then changed to Swifts (SMS), followed by RMs on Saturday only and then Fleetlines (DMS) on a Sunday. The week after this picture was taken the route went completely 'OPO' with DMSs.

From March 1959 the 229 formed an important link between Woolwich and Orpington and ran via Erith, Bexleyheath and Sidcup with the garages at the latter two providing the allocation. From May 1977 the route was revised to run between Bexleyheath and Farnborough. RM741 is seen in Farnborough High Street on 20 May 1982. Note the shop awnings that were once a common sight in many high streets.

A busy scene is depicted outside Manor House station in Seven Sisters Road on 22 July 1978. RMs 72 and 1225 occupy the bus stand, whilst Fleetline DMS1408 is resigned to waiting in the middle of the road. Route 230 only commenced running in June 1973 with a thirty-eight-minute running time between Stratford and Manor House. Six RMs were provided on Mon–Sat, although RTs had to deputise in 1976 due to a shortage of RMs.

For many years route 237 was operated by single-deck buses, with the last incumbents being Bristol LH types, from April 1977. However, in January 1978, the route was revised to run between Shepherds Bush Green and Sunbury Village with RMs. RM565 is seen in Green Street at Sunbury on 9 February 1980. The route was converted to 'OPO' Metrobus operation in February 1987.

The 243 was a trolleybus replacement route that commenced operation in July 1961. It was operated by Routemasters from its inception until August 1985, when Metrobuses took over. RML2540 is seen at Tottenham Green, heading north on the A10, on 22 July 1978. Its home garage was just around the corner in Philip Lane.

The 243A was the Sunday variant of the 243 when the southern terminus was Liverpool Street, vice the Mon–Sat terminus of Holborn Circus. The route required ten RMLs from Stamford Hill (SF) garage. RML2705 was caught in Bishopsgate, in problem mode, on 15 October 1978. Two weeks later the allocation was split evenly between Tottenham (AR) and Stamford Hill (SF). Many a Wimpy meal was consumed on these frequent trips to London.

The 253 was another trolleybus replacement route and had an allocation of fifty-two Routemasters on Mon–Fri from Holloway (HT) garage, when first introduced in February 1961. Three garages had a hand in the route when RMs 65 and 496 were caught on camera in Clapton Road, alongside Clapton Pond, on 11 March 1978. Scania Metropolitan MS4 famously took a dip in the pond on 13 August 1973, whilst working on the S2.

The theme of trolleybus replacement routes continues with this view of RM64 in Hammersmith Grove on 5 May 1980. Latterly operated by three different garages, depending on the day of the week, RM64 was one of eight buses provided by Stonebridge Park (SE) garage on Mon–Fri. Metrobuses took over in February 1985 and the route was cut back to Golders Green in June 2003.

When this photograph was taken on Saturday 22 July 1978, the 262 was largely worked by the DM/DMS Fleetline types and was only supplemented by a handful of RMLs from Leyton (T) garage on a Saturday. RML2714 is seen in Greengate Street, close to West Ham (WH) garage.

The opening of the Brent Cross Shopping Centre, in early 1976, was responsible for redefining the pattern of bus routes in the Cricklewood and Hendon localities. Among the routes affected was the 266 from Hammersmith. The crew of RM1779 take a breather before setting out from Hammersmith Grove on 16 June 1979. The buildings on either side of the road have now all been replaced by more modern structures.

One of the northern extremities of London Transport's red bus operations was the village of Hammond Street (near Flamstead End), which was reached via route 279 from Holloway (Finsbury Park on Sunday). Even on a Saturday the route required forty RMs. However, it was cut back to Smithfield from 28 October 1978, with a resultant reduction in allocation of sixteen buses. RM1050 is seen in Hammond Street Road, opposite the junction of Oaklands Road, one week before the route alteration.

Route 279A was introduced on 10 March 1973 and initially ran between Lower Edmonton and Liverpool Street on Sundays only. However, when this picture was taken of RMs 430 and 232, in Hertford Road, at Lower Edmonton, on 19 April 1982, the route had been extended northwards to Hammond Street. To the right is Tramway Avenue, at the end of which was situated Edmonton (EM) garage.

Route 281 was a replacement for trolleybus route 601, which disappeared with the final group of trolleybus routes on 9 May 1962. Originally running between Tolworth Broadway and Twickenham station, it was extended to Hounslow bus station in October 1965. RM1152 is seen with RML2305 for company at Hounslow on 24 February 1979. The route was exclusively operated by Fulwell (FW) garage.

The unique rear-engined Routemaster, FRM1, is seen in Potters Bar High Street on 19 February 1975 on its assigned local route 284. Conceived in 1964 there is paper evidence to suggest it may have been the original intention to build three of the type. It eventually entered service in June 1967 on service 76 from Tottenham (AR) garage. It was first allocated to PB in October 1971 where it stayed until September 1976. After a stint on the Sight Seeing Tour it was retired in 1983 and is now preserved.

The 298 was a modest route that required just five RMs from Palmers Green (AD) garage. Overall running time allowed for the 5.1 miles from Cockfosters station to Turnpike Lane was just twenty-five minutes. RM1959 is seen in Green Lanes at Palmers Green on 11 March 1978. It was withdrawn from LT service in May 1986 and was last reported as being at a theme park in Barcelona in the mid-1990s.

The 298A ran in parallel with the 298 for all but the last section of route, when it deviated at Southgate to follow Chase Road to Oakwood. It was the highest-numbered red bus route operated by Routemasters at the time. Palmers Green's RM1357 is seen at Oakwood station on 18 June 1979. The route was subsumed by the 298 in September 1980.